Life through a pen

Kate Young

Presentation by *BookLeaf Publishing*

Web: www.bookleafpub.com

E-mail: info@bookleafpub.com

ISBN: 9789357441834

First edition 2023

For mum.

*The creator of amazing stories, the sharer
of some amazing adventures and the person
who helped to kick start my love of poetry.*

ACKNOWLEDGEMENT

With thanks to my family, my husband Mike and our two boys Dylan and Owen for their determined push to encourage me to go over the publishing cliff edge!
With thanks also to my wonderful parents who introduced to the world of poetry and gave me the confidence to feel like I had something worthwhile to say.

PREFACE

This little collection started as a challenge to myself to make sense of the endless pieces of paper I have dotted around our house! Little moments of life reflections, notes to remind me of moments passed, or feelings that needed to be laid bare, all captured in scribbled note form.

I have written poems since the age of six, using them as a form of emotional release and as an aid to working through life's experiences. I've always felt that writing down a little bit of who we are and how we think can help to heal wounds, renew hope, create humour and above all else, give another form of connection to those around us.

This set of poems represents just a small section of the over-spill from my perhaps too crammed brain; but in reading it, I hope that it reassures the reader that we are all a bit vulnerable, all capable of being the best and worst of ourselves, and above all else, all able to take the leap of putting our world out there for others to read! I

Tree mediation

Truncated discussion took place last night;
The Branches all met to convey and compare.
Some barked frustration, afraid they'd be blown
aside.
Some suggested taking a leaf from each other's
books.
Others started to twig that there may be another
way.
Eventually, consensus and hope took some root.
Under the canopy of inter-connected shelter,
Together they saw the wood for the trees.
This path we take is just the beginning..blowing
in the breeze.

Y ddau Fachgen Cymreig
(The two Welsh boys).

Two boys walked home together,
Muddied from spoils of play.
Passed the Miner's cottage,
At the end of a summer's day.

Each boy carried their mighty sword,
well chosen from branches dis-guarded.
Knights of their own round table,
Brave, adventurous, kind-hearted.

The eldest told a story,
Of Dragons of passion and red.
The youngest loved this chosen tale.
'The land of my fathers', he said.

Along passed the castle ruins,
Where they conquered a turret each.
Then the embattled rugby fields
Where the masters of scrums can teach.

Over the bridge on the River,
To their own Kingdom of home.
Discarded swords at the ready
For next they should choose to roam.

Sky black as ink, tucked up in bed,
The youngest asked, 'are Dragon's a myth?'
Arms reaching down to kiss goodnight
The eldest whispered, 'No, Cymru am Byth'.

Lost and found

I lost myself again today
Mis-placed among the chaos
No time to take a proper look
I'm completely at a loss!

I think I may be buried
Under the list of 'to do',
Perhaps hidden under work papers
Or maybe left in the loo?

Possibly somewhere in the car
Under the piles of washing?
Caught up in a 'message group'
Symptoms of always rushing!

One day I'll find myself again.
Carve out some time to look.
Create a calm space all my own
In the safety of my nook.

Space in-between

Breathing in, breathing out,
The brief window of pause
Before we next take action.
A quiet resting place,
For momentary reflection.
To temporarily stay
As molecules of calm
Binding time lived together.
The space in-between
Where we can be us.

Therapy room

6

A session was called
For a friday night.
The issue reached crisis,
So, timing was right.
Those who attended,
Friends long known.
Weathered strong bonds,
All woven and sewn.
Wine was in order
Easing stings in the tail.
Hugs are prescribed,
So treatment can't fail.
Solutions were shared,
As hours ticked by
Laughter and tears
The question of 'why'?
The session drew closed
Less deepening gloom,
A successful gathering
Of the Therapy Room.

Good grief.

I still talk to you
Almost every new day
Each pause feels forever
Since life ebbed away.

Hearing your voice inside
Living life as prepared
Recalling those adventures
All the guidance you shared.

It's the simplest things
That I still miss so much
Being alone together
Smiles, a gentle hand touch.

Though the days will pass,
I know that this is true.
As I grow wiser in myself
I will always carry you.

Tea break

8

Warmest of nectars, homely,
Encased in ceramic edge.
Golden in colour, cupped between hands
Carefully blended, not to overstew
The simplest perfections
Of the humble home brew.

Fly like a bird

To fly like a bird,
The freedom it can give.
A bird's eye view
The freshest perspective.
The chance to change scenery
The space to take flight.
Directions will alter
For some, clearer insight.
Dangers can be evaded, but
Risks still enabled.
To fly like a bird,
The freedom it can give.
The envy of those grounded
Oh, the stories they live!

The helpful dilemma

Help can be helpful,
Unless it is not...
If help has been offered,
Should we take what we've got?
Is it right to impose help
If they may not have asked?
Is it always helpful,
To set helpful tasks?

Perhaps its that helping
Is often the right thing to do,
As long as the help,
Is truly for them, not just for you.

Insomnia

I - instant hot chocolate made and consumed
N - Natural scented oil pillows all perfumed
S -Sleep masks purchased and duly applied
O -Open book read until face bleary eyed.
M - Morning alarm clock set for the rise
N - Night lights off, just starlight skies.
I - Items all done, no further actions to take
A-Alas, all for nought, I am still here awake!

The measure of worth?

If worth is a measure,
Where should we start?
Sewn up with strength,
Lines of scars on a heart.
The trigger of judgement,
Leads to power devolved.
On the surface calm waters,
Deep within, cracks unresolved.
Self love as a balm
Although known as a cure,
Is sometimes misplaced
Though the intention is pure.
If worth is the measure
We may all be lost.
Unless those that bring love
Soothe opinions' sharp frost!

Pointed debate

Do get to the point
At least, try and be clear
If the point we are noting,
Is either far or quite near?
If the point being made
Brings together views joint
Then, I urge with a plea
Please DO get to the point!

Tides of love

As a wave crashes inwards
I land on your shore
Arms embracing, safe once more.

As a wave crashes outwards,
I am pulled from your door
Distance gathering, lost once more.

As the tide ebbs and flows,
Waves of love, dip and soar.
A Constant rhythm, begins once more.

Hands of time

Once, tiny hands gripped so tightly,
Legs wrapped in blankets all warm.
Overwhelmed, new and dependent,
Vulnerable in their newborn form.

Once, small hands held on firmly,
Legs stepping out in sturdy boots.
Giggling, exploring a world outside
With puddles and leaves in cahoots.

Once, young hands brushed lightly,
Legs confident, striding to school.
Friendships, hobbies the new distraction
Other's assistance no longer a tool.

Once, adult hands stood independent
Long legs marching to and from life.
Work, love and home form foundations
Returning for comforts from strife.

Once, tiny hands griped tightly,
Legs wrapped up in blankets all warm.
Adult hands, now able, steady others,
Life repeats, in this caring form.

The River

Like a clear skinned serpent,
It winds a path down.
Down through the valley,
On into the town.
Meandering lazily,
lapping at playful knees,
Birds dart down to fish on
the warm hazy summer breeze.
Then charged to power onward
by winter's torrents of rain,
It bursts out at our coastline,
Land's loss, the ocean's gain.

Sibling carer manifesto

When I grow up,
I will live each moment,
As if they're all gifts to cherish,
...Just like my brother does.

When I grow up,
I will hold no resentments,
Though prejudice surrounds us,
...Just like my brother does.

When I grow up,
I will push boundaries further
Where barriers block opportunity,
...Just like my brother does.

When I grow up,
I will use humour as healing
Shining smiles through the darkness
...Just like my brother does.

When I grow up,
I will strive to make the world
kinder, fairer, by example
...because that's what my brother has taught me.

The Opportune moment

Listen not for the cheering
But for the chance to take part.
Listen not for the giggling
But for the joke at the start.
Listen not for the footfall
But for the shoes being laced.
Listen not for the verdict
But for the option to taste.
Listen not for their adventures
But for the chance to dig deep.
Listen not for the right time
But for the moment to leap!

The seasons of living

In my spring years I shall be green with naivety,
Make daisy chains in fields, play games with
friends,
and not care much for the weather's change.
School will be consuming, days will feel endless
The road ahead long, stretched out to be lived.

In my summer years I shall have found my true
colours,
Energy high, having picnics with friends
and care only for weather that stops children's
play.
Work will be consuming, days will fill faster
The road partially travelled, but with much still
ahead.

In my autumn years I shall carry sunset's warm
glow,
Selfishly slower, having lunch out with friends
and care only for weather that causes delays in
our play.
Work will be less, kids will be grown,
The road now well travelled, still has a distance
to go.

In my winter years I shall have hair that reflects
winters tones,
Gently paced, having tea out with friends,
and care only for weather to get out for the day.
Work will be memories, kids will have kids of
their own.
The road now perhaps shorter, the distance left
still unknown.